Nightcrawler's Missives

Dwight Carlson

These Missives are the result of a hack into the e-mails between one of Satan's generals, Beelzebub, and his understudy, Nightcrawler.

Hack #1

WESTBOW
PRESS®
A DIVISION OF THOMAS NELSON
& ZONDERVAN

Scripture quotations taken from the New American Standard Bible®,
Copyright © 1960, 1962, 1963, 1968, 1971, 1972, 1973, 1975, 1977, 1995
by The Lockman Foundation. Used by permission. (www.Lockman.org)

WestBow Press books may be ordered through booksellers or by contacting:

WestBow Press
A Division of Thomas Nelson & Zondervan
1663 Liberty Drive
Bloomington, IN 47403
www.westbowpress.com
1 (866) 928-1240

Because of the dynamic nature of the Internet, any web addresses or
links contained in this book may have changed since publication and
may no longer be valid. The views expressed in this work are solely those
of the author and do not necessarily reflect the views of the publisher,
and the publisher hereby disclaims any responsibility for them.

Any people depicted in stock imagery provided by Thinkstock are models,
and such images are being used for illustrative purposes only.
Certain stock imagery © Thinkstock.

ISBN: 978-1-5127-5026-3 (sc)
ISBN: 978-1-5127-5028-7 (hc)
ISBN: 978-1-5127-5027-0 (e)

Library of Congress Control Number: 2016911662

Print information available on the last page.

WestBow Press rev. date: 11/17/2016

Dedicated to Don Rhodes,
who stimulated my revisiting *The Screwtape Letters*
after seldom looking at them for over sixty years.

Contents

Acknowledgments

I want to thank many individuals who reviewed the manuscript carefully and made many helpful suggestions. Some gave reasonable counsel that I chose not to follow—for that I take total responsibility. In particular, I want to thank Michael Alvarez, Greg Carlson, Bob Li, Tess Howe, John Notehelfer, Fritz Ridenour, Nancy Thomason, Charissa Wood, and Susan Wood for their helpful comments. Cover sketch is by Roger Bradfield and the photo by Tom Ginn.

Introduction

My brother, Dr. Paul Carlson, gave me my copy of *The Screwtape Letters* as a Christmas present in 1954. Paul later went to the Congo as a medical missionary and was killed there in 1964. A friend of mine, Don Rhodes, recently gave a series on C. S. Lewis, and this stimulated my renewed interest in *The Screwtape Letters,* which resulted in my writing these missives.

After serving as an enlisted person in the navy, practicing both internal medicine and psychiatry, and having been a lifelong student of the Bible, I have seen and heard almost everything—the good, the bad, and the ugly. My hope is to use satire and humor to grab your attention, shine light on areas that are often in the shadows, and jar you to consider some adjustments with ultimate beneficial results for all.

Anyone who has read *The Screwtape Letters* by C. S. Lewis will immediately be aware that the *style* of writing in this book is similar to his. Other writers have used a similar technique over the years, namely Peter Kreeft in *The Snakebite Letters* and Randy Alcorn in *Lord Foulgrin's Letters.*

On the cover I claim, "These missives are the result of a hack into the e-mails between one of Satan's generals, Beelzebub, and his understudy, Nightcrawler." Of course, this is fiction; however, this book is my attempt to capture some of the communication that might take place between the self-centered, fallen angels, who are not only alive and well but also acting as the proponents of evil, actively trying to cause you and me to sin against God and those around us. We should not focus too much attention on Satan, but I fear in this century we are almost totally unaware that we have such a powerful and active adversary trying to draw us away from our loving heavenly Father and his will for our lives.

I want it to be very clear I am not personally endorsing many of the things advocated in these e-mails; I am attempting to write from the point of view of the evil forces of Satan and from his perspective of things—so you can't trust everything "they" say.

I believe that Satan and the forces of evil are, unfortunately, very active and at work on planet earth. So this is intended to be a humorous way to get your attention and at the same time, make some very serious points that, in my opinion, we all need to consider. After your initial reaction to this material, whatever it is, ask yourself, "What can I learn from knowing a little more about the tactics my enemy is using so as to make me more proactive for *God* and *good*?" The scriptures, in fact, encourage us to be aware of Satan's schemes, so hopefully this will allow you to take a look at some of the enemy's current tactics.[1]

However, let me caution you; there are two extremes to be avoided. The first is denying or minimizing the existence and active work of Satan on planet earth. The second is an excessive focus on Satan and his tactics.

So I trust you will initially be humored or maybe even upset by this "read," but then you will give serious thought to the material and as you are able, move to appropriate corrective action.

At the end of each letter, there are some questions for your personal or group consideration. Actually, if you go through this book with a group of individuals and discuss the issues raised, you will find you and others will get the most out of this material.

Missive 1

Cartoons of Mohamed

My Dear Nightcrawler:

I want to commend you for instilling in the minds of cartoonists in the free world that they should be able to draw cartoons of anything they want. There should be total freedom of speech or written expression—period. We see big ears on presidents and bushy, combed forward hair on, what's his name—ah, Donald Trump, I think it is—and all kinds of sarcastic things portrayed in the daily newspapers. So what's wrong with a cartoon of the Prophet Mohamed? And you shrewdly promoted this attitude and have gotten magazines to take a strong stand on expressing their right—freedom of the press.

At the same time, I noticed you cunningly showing these cartoons of the prophet to some radical Muslims, and naturally they were irate. Like gasoline and matches, you have created an explosion. The result: some cartoonists got killed. Now both sides are indignant at the inappropriate actions of the other! That's right where we want them!

I have been around for thousands of years, and there are still a few things I don't understand about these creatures our enemy created called *Homo sapiens*. They know certain things will be provocative to others, and they do them anyway—I guess to prove they can. They don't seem to realize that such behavior is a big asset to our cause of creating chaos, and we have been only too glad to promote the idea among humans—"don't put any boundaries on me ... don't fence me in."

I suspect there are some distorted things that a cartoonist could do with most earthlings' mothers to put on the cover of a magazine, which would get one's dander up! I could picture some depictions of Christ and Mary or the Pope that I think most earthlings of the Christian faith would find very offensive. In the United States some might even get out their 45s! How about some cartoons about Moses? Bet that would fire up some Orthodox tempers!

Earthlings need to consider: Is there a point where one's right to freedom of expression violates another's rights? Does the neighbor next door have the right to have a party till 3:00 a.m. with a boom box blasting away? At some point, it seems even from my down-under perspective and even in a free society, one person's rights might cross with what another person considers his or her rights. Even I, as one of the devil's chief officers, think there is—but don't you dare quote me on that!

Nightcrawler, sometimes these humans baffle me, but let's take advantage of it whenever we can egg on the cartoonists' drawing—standing up for their rights—that is, until we stir someone up to mow them down!

Your Cordial Assessor,
Uncle Beelzebub

For Your Consideration

1. Is it appropriate to have any limit on freedom of speech, cartoons, etc.? Should anything go? How might a passage like Colossians 4:6 apply, which says: "Let your speech always be with grace, seasoned, as it were, with salt, so that you may know how you should respond to each person"? If you think some limitation is appropriate, what parameters would you suggest?

2. As the scribe of this book, I attend weekly what I consider a good evangelical church, yet I don't think I have heard a reference to Satan or the devil at church in the last twenty years. When is the last time you heard any reference to Satan or the devil at church? What do you think about the emphasis, or lack of it, on Satan and his works? Is even the whole idea of a Satan or the devil passé?

3. Is it possible to have an excessive interest in the evil forces of Satan, and if so, what are the consequences of such an interest? Is it possible to minimize the role of Satan in our personal lives and world, and what are the consequences of that extreme? On a scale of zero to ten—with zero denying the existence of Satan and ten, seeing him behind every rock—where would you put yourself, your friends, and your church? What is ideal, and what would that look like?

4. Second Corinthians 2:11 says, "In order that no advantage be taken of us by Satan; for we are not ignorant of his schemes." It seems that this verse is saying we need to be aware of Satan's techniques to adequately combat him. Is that your understanding of the verse, and if so, what are the schemes we need to be aware of?

5. Jesus confronted and dealt with a physical Satan during his time on the earth. You may remember in Matthew 4:1–11 a very real Satan appeared in the flesh to tempt Christ three times. The scribe of these missives believes Satan could appear in flesh today and tempt us. If that is true, why do you think it is to his advantage *not* to appear in the flesh? Or, does he appear in the flesh and we don't recognize who he is?

Missive 2

Drones

My Dear Nightcrawler:

I have been fascinated by what those earthlings can do with modern technology: computers, the Internet, cell phones, and even artificial intelligence. There is no telling where this might end. Earthlings invent them for good, wholesome purposes, but before they are off the production line, we have already figured out how to use them for our purposes. We actually can have someone sit in Moscow and rob a New York bank of millions! We can addict people to pornography without them ever leaving their house. Amazing—what a gift!

Over the Internet we can recruit wives for key radicalized Muslim leaders half the world away, and we can find and encourage disgruntled, confused individuals to commit acts of terror. It doesn't cost us a penny, and their authorities are scrambling to determine who is radicalized. Can you think of a more ideal set-up?

But like all advances, they can be used by us or by the enemy. We have to look for how we can turn what looks like a defeat for us into a win. Take, for example, the United States using drones.

At first we sent an urgent alert all the way down to Satan to somehow stop the drone project.

Then Satan himself pointed out that many a missile fired by an American drone at one of our operatives misses its intended target, and in the process it kills many innocent individuals—sometimes as many as 128 individuals by one missile.[2] This slaughter is creating numerous recruits who want revenge against the "Great Satan" that has killed their fathers, mothers, siblings, relatives, and friends. Every one of these innocent individuals has thirty to fifty friends and relatives ready to be jihadists who now have become archenemies of the American imperialists. This has become a fertile recruiting tool and has produced numerous new enemies with each drone strike. Nightcrawler, this is fueling the very radicals the United States is trying to destroy—and all we have to do is sit back and watch the fireworks! Keep the United States firing those drones—it's the radical Muslims' and our best recruiting tool yet! They kill one and create three in its wake—pretty good odds!

Let me cite just one example that occurred in Pakistan in October 2012 when eight-year-old Nabeela ventured out with her sixty-eight-year-old grandmother Mammana Bibi to work in the fields. Little Nabeela saw her grandmother blown up in front of her eyes by a US drone. Now Nabeela, everyone in her community, and her extended family live in terror that at any time they might be killed by a US drone. Some even have trouble sleeping at night—post-traumatic stress disorder in spades. They see the United States as "the Great Satan." Amnesty International considers this a possible war crime. As of 2014 the United States had launched over five hundred such drone strikes. Do the math—figure out how many enemies they have created against "the Great Satan."

Nightcrawler, I wonder how Americans would like this method of trial and prosecution. A suspected bad guy lives in the duplex next to you. There is no formal charge, no trial, and no defense. At 3:00 a.m. tonight, a missile goes through his roof and takes out a few others with him—and maybe someone from your family. Think of the rage that would generate in the community! That's the kind of justice the United States is meting out, and those US citizens are sitting at home watching the horrible things the jihadists are doing on their TVs every night. Yet they don't even begin to appreciate how they might be contributing to the carnage!

So cheer up, Nightcrawler, and put some of your fears to rest. "The Great Satan"—and I don't mean our boss—is doing our work for us!

Your Cordial Assessor,
Uncle Beelzebub

For Your Consideration

1. How would you rate the positive and negative value of drones?

2. Is there any legitimate basis for Middle Easterners to see the United States as "the Great Satan"? Elaborate on the basis for your answer.

3. When innocent individuals are killed or when collateral property is destroyed, should the United States pay compensation or be tried for war crimes? How about when we bomb a hospital? If your answer is no, on what basis should the United States support other individuals or nations being tried for war crimes?

4. What is your opinion about the United States using drones to kill individuals? If you were president of the United States, would you continue their use? Would you alter it in some way? Would you ever consider carpet bombing? Christ said in Matthew 5:38–39: "You have heard that it was said, 'AN EYE FOR AN EYE, AND A TOOTH FOR A TOOTH.' "But I say to you, do not resist him who is evil; but whoever slaps you on your right cheek, turn to him the other also." Romans 12:17 says: "Never pay back evil for evil to anyone." How do you reconcile verses like this and the reality of jihad?

5. Do you think the scribe's example of using a drone in the United States is a fair comparison?

6. What position do you think the United States should take on drones?

Missive 3

Bush Two's War!

My Dear Nightcrawler:

Scuttlebutt has it that our supreme leader himself planted the thought in Mr. Cheney's and Bush Two's heads that they would get a lot of kudos for destroying Saddam's regime and give the people of Iraq DEMOCRACY—spelled in capital letters.

The idea planted in their minds was that Saddam had some major faults—like killing some of his own people—together with the fantasy that Iraqis wanted Saddam overthrown. The seed of an idea was then watered by the "obvious" truth that any country, given the opportunity, would jump at the chance of having a democracy—especially if given to them on a silver platter! Well, maybe in a bomb crater! Then democracy would ripple through the Middle East, and Mr. Cheney and Bush Two would go down in history with kudos. Of course there is one very minor assumption here: that a Middle Eastern country with an ancient tribal culture and two warring factions of their religion would want and be able to function as a democracy. Never mind that Cheney and Bush Two didn't have the foggiest about what they were getting the world into.

Initially there was one problem—convincing Congress and the American people that we should go to war. Then he planted another brilliant thought in their minds. Colin Powell has a stellar reputation—send him to do their dirty work and convince Congress and the American people that we should go to war. They trust him.

As predicted, Colin Powell forgot that he had taken off his uniform and with it should have shed the standard knee-jerk reaction—"Yes sir," "Can do, sir"—to one's superior. He had been trained well. Like a dutiful solider, he searched until he found something he could use; and sure enough, with his stellar reputation and some shaky facts, Congress and the American people bought the war, hook, line, and sinker. And sink her it did.

The world watched in "shock and awe" as innocent Iraqis died and their city was used for kindling the biggest Fourth of July fireworks in history. The only thing that Cheney and Bush Two got right was the "shock and awe."

Nightcrawler, we haven't had a break like this since the Third Reich. Iraq is now like Humpty Dumpty. Once there was "shock and awe," and now all the West's military horses and all the king's military men and money will not be able to put Humpty Dumpty back together again. Sorry, Humpty Dumpty, Middle East, and the entire world!

Saddam had many faults, as do most leaders in the world today. However, he gave a significant degree of stability to the Middle East. Once both Muslims and Christians could worship safely—now they both are blown up as they worship. It has become our choicest breeding ground for our groups spewing out hatred, terror, and death. Now no one is safe—especially Christians, but also many Muslims. Most of the Christians have left, eking out an existence in some foreign country that doesn't want refugees.

Nightcrawler, we clearly won this one—we just need to keep milking it for all we can get out of it—and mark my words, it will be a lot for decades to come—unless He calls curtains on the world first. Then it is all over for us—dread that day! But until then let's enjoy the ride!

Your Cordial Assessor,
Uncle Beelzebub

For Your Consideration

1. Do you think it is preposterous to think of Satan being behind the Iraq war or other such world events? How about Hitler and WWII? What about ISIS? Would that include any of the "free world's" activities?

2. God's word tells us to pray for our leaders. Unfortunately, many of us neglect this, and if so do we bear some, or a lot, of the responsibility for the actions of our leaders and country?

3. Is there a take-home message from this missive? If so, what is it?

4. Do we in the free world, especially in the United States, have any responsibility to all the refugees from the Middle East? What about those who stay in the Middle East but whose homes and businesses have been destroyed?

5. Do you think "resisting the devil" is more difficult today than it was fifty years ago? What about one or two thousand years ago? What is the rationale for your answer?

Missive 4

News Cycle and Polarized Media

Dear Nightcrawler:

I will start out with the things you have done right. I did learn a thing or two from some of the earthlings' books, such as *How to Win Friends and Influence People!*

Your developing the twenty-four-hour news cycle on radio and TV was an ingenious idea. But adding the Internet and cell phone has tacked on another whole layer of influence—keeping the enemy's followers glued to the latest news or more accurately, the latest piece of slander, and it's all right there, at their fingertips. These new technologies are so cheap that the average person anywhere in the world, even in some undeveloped, Timbuktu places, can be totally immersed in the "truths" and "facts" that we help distort and manipulate.

You see a shack in the third world that doesn't have running water or a toilet; but they have a TV antenna sticking out of their thatched roof and the kids running around half-naked, texting on their cell phones. You're getting them trapped in a powerful addiction that we can build upon—*and communicate to.* How sweet is that!

The idiot earthlings listen to their biased news outlets and parrot what they hear. Not infrequently, commentators are mean to those opposing their prejudices. The Muslim world has their media influence too—and, for sure, it is as one sided as the so-called free world's. I have to chuckle every time I see "free world" in print. If only they knew how entangled they are in their own biases. They no longer listen to both sides of an issue, study the facts, and evaluate the reliability of the sources before deciding where the truth lies.

With your brilliant idea of having "conservative" and "liberal" radio, TV, and newspapers, people keep reinforcing their already biased opinions. The earthlings no longer listen to each other—and that's great news for us. They listen to one side, accept it hook, line, and sinker, and parrot it to the next person. In fact, some of them are concluding the only place they can get reliable news is on their one-sided station or newspaper. If only they knew! When talking to someone new, they listen—that is, they only listen long enough to pigeonhole the other party into one camp or the other "they're either for us or agin' us." Once they know that, they either commiserate, attack, or avoid the subject altogether. That way they never have to engage their own minds at all. If they differ and do talk to each other, they talk over one another or argue so that any sane person would want to flee.

Fortunately, there aren't too many sane people left. A sane discussion is no longer possible, not only by our followers—which is okay—but your great achievement has been to so permeate this mind-set and way of reacting into the enemy's people that they have fallen into the same pathetic communication style.

Nightcrawler, I am seldom at a loss for words, but I don't know how I could improve on what you have done. Just don't let the enemy's followers get wind of this. If they do—have them attack the source!

Your Cordial Assessor,
Uncle Beelzebub

For Your Consideration

1. Do you think there is any problem with getting most or all your news from sources that are known to lean to either the liberal or conservative side? Discuss the advantages and disadvantages.

2. What is the source of the news that you read/listen to or watch? Do you listen/watch/read some on both the right and the left?

3. In your opinion are newscasters ever "cruel" to those they interview? What do you think of this? What are the long-term results?

Missive 5

Prevent Dialogue

Dear Nightcrawler,

As I wander around, I notice another thing that is happening on planet earth. I don't know if you fostered the inability of dumb earthlings to have a meaningful exchange of ideas or they fell into it on their own—without any help from us. You know they sometimes do foolish things like that—the idiots. Regardless of how it started, upright followers of our enemy who have differing views on matters such as politics or religious issues don't really dialogue with each other. They seem to have an unspoken rule: "We don't talk about such issues." On Facebook many avoid expressing their differing opinions because they want to be liked and not ridiculed for taking an unpopular stance. Actually, Nightcrawler, it is to our advantage to keep them dumbed down! It does take a lot of knowledge about the issues most of them think they have—but many don't—and self-discipline and maturity to have a meaningful, civil, give-and-take discussion on important, controversial issues. I don't know where the idea came from, but let's not question it and, on the contrary, foster it. Some have tried to discuss these things and have been so beaten up that they decided, "Never again." That is a sad commentary for them, but so good for us! But don't breathe a word of any of this to them.

Even more than politics, you have spread this notion among his followers and the rest of the world that various flavors of religion are often off limits for discussion. Great work! Actually this is a logical progression for the nonthinking person. Of all people, his followers ought to be able to have a mature, adult dialogue about such important issues as we are referring to—but don't tell them that!

These earthlings are just like three-year-olds in a playpen fighting over whose ball it is when there are ten other interesting objects to play with—but no, each has to play with the ball now. Two minutes from now they will have a tug-of-war over whose fire truck it is. Stupid earthlings, especially supposedly mature followers of the enemy, act no better than quarreling three-year-olds now fighting over whose teddy bear it is.

Furthermore, when it comes to critical political or social/moral issues, the substance of the instant news media is often paper thin, no, electron thin. And many of his followers, like those who are our followers, only know the talking points. They can't have an intelligent, sane discussion because they only know the conclusion they want and don't really know the constituent material. *They think they do—but they don't.*

That is why in most of these so-called dialogues, one argues, raises his voice, talks over the other person—but for God's sake … oops, Satan's sake—somebody's sake, at all costs, don't allow them to learn how to have a mature, give-and-take discussion on these important issues. I couldn't care less about the political realm— both of their overall agendas are a pretty mixed bag—but I very much care about the spiritual. Nevertheless, keep it the way it is, because if they were to learn to have a sane dialogue about politics,

they just might apply it to moral and then spiritual issues—
something to be avoided at all costs!

Well this has gotten to be a much longer missive than I
intended.

Your Cordial Assessor,
Uncle Beelzebub

For Your Consideration

1. Are you able to have a civil, informative, give-and-take discussion with those who differ with you politically? What about spiritually?

2. Would people who see things differently from you say *you* are able to have a kind, civil, in-depth dialogue without feeling a lot of contention? Does a verse like Colossians 4:6 apply, which says: "Let your speech always be with grace, seasoned, as it were with salt, so that you might know how you should respond to each person"?

3. Is this a goal that one should pursue? Why?

4. How might you go about fostering an environment where you and others might talk about important issues on you differ? Is it possible *you* might learn something by this kind of dialogue? Would it be of value to others?

Missive 6

Porn in the Church

My Dear Nightcrawler:

As you know we have a dirty little secret, and everyone who is involved in it wants to keep it that way—from the pastor to head deacon and janitor, too. Surprising as it may seem, some outstanding women in the church also succumb to this addiction. You know, of course, that I'm referring to porn.

Now it's so easy. In the old days if someone wanted to watch porn, they had to drive to the shady side of town, or better yet a town down the road a ways, wear a trench coat, make sure no one they knew was looking, and sneak into a porn shop. Now with the marvels of the Internet, all they need to do is open up their computer and in one click, it's all there—instantly, the offering of 182 million sites clamoring for one's attention![3] Once they visit a site and watch the latest sneak show's titillating commercial, a new offering is on their inbox. It now comes to them—seeking them out—and, oh, how difficult it is for them to delete it. All they have to carefully watch for is that mother, babe, boss, or goodie two-shoe church secretary doesn't walk in on them at that inopportune moment. The Internet does all of this for us, Nightcrawler! Hurrah!

One of the enemy's leaders—a Swindoll calls it "the number one secret problem in your church"! The audacity of calling attention to one of our cherished endeavors! Anyway, how does he know? He goes on to say something like it could be eating your church alive and ruining marriages, destroying relationships, and harming youth. Duh. Just because statistics show that 64 percent of Christian men and 15 percent of Christian women view pornography at least once a month—statistics only slightly better than non-Christians! Another study conducted over five years reported 68 percent of Christian men view pornography regularly.[4]

Nightcrawler, do your best to have the leaders in every church dismiss the whole notion as a problem in other churches—certainly not theirs. After all, their upright leaders and members wouldn't stoop to such depths as being involved in porn. If there is any problem in their church, it's limited to adolescent boys. After all, "boys, will be boys," and it's a phase they will grow out of—"so let's not get sidetracked from the important task of preaching the gospel and saving lost souls." Don't let it even cross anyone's mind that there could be a porn addiction in our spiritual leaders, deacons, and elders and certainly not in any of our fine women. It may happen in other churches—but not in our church! Above all, don't let it out that many women find romantic novels more stimulating than actual porn—and for our purposes this is just as destructive to these dignified ladies.

Nightcrawler, we've a good thing going here. Don't let the enemy mess with what we've got. Porn poisons people's minds, plays havoc with marriages, and causes adultery and divorce. Keep the churches under your supervision in denial of this problem. If anyone raises it as a possible problem in their church, then they must have a personal problem with porn—otherwise why would they bring the subject up!

Your Cordial Assessor,
Uncle Beelzebub

For Your Consideration

1. How much of a problem is porn in your church? What is the basis for your answer? Do you have any idea at all as to the extent of the problem?

2. Has the problem of porn ever been preached on in your church? Should it be, or is this a subject that should be avoided? What will the older, *"sophisticated" people* in your church think if it is preached on? Should that make any difference?

3. If someone, male or female, has a problem with porn, will he or she readily know how to get help in your church?

4. If someone came to you for help—what would you do or suggest?

5. If porn is so widespread in churches, do you think every church should have some established way to help those who are struggling with this problem?

6. Do you even believe there is such a being as Satan? Does he have others that work with or for him? Consider 2 Corinthians 2:11, which says: "In order that no advantage be taken of us by Satan; for we are not ignorant of his schemes" and Revelation 12:10 tells us that Satan is "the accuser of our brethren … who accuses them before God day and night." According to these verses, how might Satan attack you? Give specific examples.

7. What do you think Satan looks like? The scriptures in 2 Corinthians 11:14 say, "Satan disguises himself as an angel of light." What might that mean? Does this give us any insight as to the types of temptations he might use against us? Explain.

8. Does it make any difference if we view a temptation as just a weakness of the flesh versus an actual demonic being tempting us? For the next few weeks, when you are tempted, maybe to lust, envy, overeat, or whatever, envision Satan personally promoting that temptation—maybe even placing the thought in your mind while the Holy Spirit is countering with caution. See if that alters your view of the temptation and how you handle it. Consider Matthew 4:3, which says, "The tempter came and said to Him," actually tempting Christ. When Christ rejected the temptation, he told Satan in Matthew 4:10, "Begone, Satan!"

9. It has been said, "If you think you can't fall into sexual sin, then you're godlier than David, stronger than Samson, and wiser than Solomon."[5]

10. The following sites offer help for those who have a problem with porn: http://www.covenanteyes.com and http://www.conquerseries.com

Missive 7

All They Want Is Meat!

Dear Nightcrawler:

Most of the time I take your word for everything—and for the most part you are trustworthy, but occasionally I wonder if you aren't trying to "pull the wool over my eyes"—to use one of them earthlings' sayings. Wool—we don't need any of that stuff to keep us warm—we've got plenty of heat where we are from.

At any rate I heard this twenty-something girl tell this usually well-informed elder at one of the enemy's prime churches that "all the guys around here want is meat."[6]

The look on the elder's face was one of total confusion.

I bent over with laughter—it sure is a good thing the earthlings don't see or hear us directly. He must have been envisioning some pork chop that the guys were all clamoring for. In sort of disbelieving disgust, the twenty-something girl said: "All they want is sex!" Totally taken back by this, all the elder could conjure up was, "Oh." He didn't have the foggiest idea of what to say to this! I think that pretty well describes the response in most churches—including their pastors and leaders! Those over sixty don't have a clue as to what is going on—or maybe they just don't want to know and admit what is going on! Then how would they deal with it if they did acknowledge the problem!

Among pastors: 43 percent have visited a pornographic site, with 21 percent doing so "a few times a year" and 6 percent "a couple times a month or more."[7] Some sources cite as high as "50% of pastors view pornography regularly.[8]

One owner of a large hotel told the scribe of these missives that one weekend when it hosted a youth pastors' conference, the revenue for the pay-per-view TV channel showing porn skyrocketed. Of course none of that means that it is happening among the staff or members of "our church"!

Nightcrawler, I commend you for how you have infiltrated the loose sexual standards of our world right into the stronghold of the enemy. It's kind of like the fox guarding the henhouse. On the other hand, we must continue to be careful that the enemy's leadership in his sanctuaries doesn't fully appreciate how far we have infiltrated their people. While they are vaguely aware of it, they choose to remain in denial as to the full extent of the problem for fear of having to deal with a problem they know they are poorly equipped to handle. Frankly, they find it very uncomfortable to deal with and would prefer to remain ignorant—so let's help them continue in their ignorance by offering all kinds of reasonable rationalizations for not doing anything.

Your very affectionate,
Uncle Beelzebub

For Your Consideration

1. What is the status of sexual promiscuity in your church? Are you qualified to answer this question? If you are not, how could you go about finding answer? Would an anonymous questionnaire ever be appropriate?

2. How important might it be for church leadership to know how pervasive porn viewing is among those who attend their church?

3. Do you think your church leadership would just as soon not know the answer to these questions? Discuss.

4. How should your church handle this problem? How about the church worldwide?

Missive 8

Rebecca, George, and Tom

Dear Uncle Beelzebub:

I think I should be able to brag a little and tell my dear old uncle of a recent success. Rebecca and George are key leaders in their young people's ministry at church. They have dated for two years and three months ago announced their engagement. Since they got engaged, George has been putting a lot of pressure on Rebecca to have sex, saying, "After all, we'll soon be married." She has yielded a few times, followed with tremendous guilt and a giant argument. Christmas Day they were together and he pressed her for sex; she refused, and the subsequent argument led to George asking for his ring back. He left with ring in hand, and she was left with a migraine. She hasn't heard from him since. She has been crying herself to sleep every night since then.

New Year's day, on the spur of the moment, she went to a singles bar to watch the Rose Bowl game. She normally doesn't like that environment but needed some sort of relief from her pain. After a couple of drinks, she got into the spirit of things and met this neat guy, Tom. A few hours later she found herself back in her apartment, in bed with Tom. To say she had a hangover the next day would be an understatement.

Tom went to Sunday school as a kid but hasn't had much use for religion since then. Uncle Beelzebub, I knew this was a relationship I could use to inflict more pain on Rebecca, so I encouraged her to invite him to church to keep the relationship going! She did, and he accepted—not because he wanted to go, but it was a small price to pay for Rebecca. Sunday they went to church, and they ended up sitting right in front of Mr. Jones, Rebecca's uncle. During the service it appeared to Tom that Mr. Jones was eyeing him in a sort of disapproving way. As they left the church, Rebecca introduced her uncle to Tom. Mr. Jones was as cool as an ice cube, probably because of the recent breakup of her engagement and then Rebecca dating someone else so soon— what kind of an example was that to the young people's group? Anyway, Mr. Jones was hoping George and Rebecca would get back together.

All the way back to the apartment Tom expressed his anger at the holier-than-thou-attitude of Mr. Jones and to think he was her uncle! Tom kept saying he would never go back to church again, period!

The day ended with Tom and Rebecca getting into a big argument and Tom storming out, saying the relationship was over—she would not see him again!

Rebecca has been so devastated she has had a hard time functioning at work.

Any suggestions, Uncle? You have had a lot more experience in situations like this than I have had.

Your Most Appreciative Understudy,
Nightcrawler

For Your Consideration

1. Do you think this is a realistic scenario in good churches today? Elaborate on your answer.

2. How much pressure do young people in your church face to have sex?

3. Should Rebecca be concerned about Tom's eternal destiny? What are the risks she faces in this situation?

Missive 9

Tom's Lost!

Dear Nightcrawler:

No problem! Keep putting into Rebecca's mind that Tom is "*lost*"—going to hell with a big H. She certainly doesn't want that to happen. It is her sole responsibility to try and see him "*saved*" from you-know-what! Encourage her to invite him over for his favorite beef stew served in her most sexy dress. Then you can sit back and enjoy the evening!

Your Experienced Uncle,
Beelzebub

For Your Consideration

1. What do you think of Beelzebub's advice?

2. How would you advise Rebecca? What is the risk/benefit of each possible approach Rebecca might take?

3. In an earlier missive I suggested you change your paradigm and view each temptation as if Satan, himself, was putting in your mind the temptation toward evil and the Holy Spirit was countering that, telling you to resist Satan's temptation. Have you done this? What are your conclusions now about this paradigm shift?

Missive 10

Rebecca Serves Meat

Uncle Beelzebub:

I thought you were out of your mind putting all those Christian ideas into Rebecca's mind. I thought that kind of stuff only came from our enemy—but to say I was surprised is an understatement. So we can plant "godly" ideas into people's minds for the wrong reason!

You're a genius. Tom jumped at the invitation. Rebecca served dinner in her most seductive dress, and he ended up getting more than just dinner. Rebecca's later confused feelings were somewhat placated by Tom's willingness to go to church with her the following Sunday. There was something in Rebecca's life that was intriguing to Tom.

Uncle, I was feeling on top of the world until they went to church and Tom heard for the first time in his life that God loves him, wants to save him from his sin, and for him to avoid spending eternity with us in, you know where, but to spend it in God's marvelous splendor. He even talked to Mr. Jones afterward and after a long discussion prayed the so-called sinner's prayer.

Rebecca was elated as they enjoyed Sunday lunch—that is until she found out Tom was married, though separated from his wife of five years and their three-year-old son.

Rebecca and Tom see each other almost daily, and Tom initiates wanting to read "the Book"—you know the one I mean. He has all kinds of "God" questions for Rebecca to answer.

Uncle, what advice would you give me now—this has taken a twist I didn't expect?

Your Understudy,
Nightcrawler

For Your Consideration

1. What is your reaction to this missive?

2. Should Rebecca keep seeing Tom? Explain the rationale for your answer. What are the possible pitfalls?

3. Does *Satan* ever plant seemingly godly ideas into our minds for the wrong reason? If your answer is yes, can you give an example?

4. Sexual promiscuity is rampant in the free world; to what extent do you think it has invaded our "good" churches? To what extent has it involved your church? What are the advantages and disadvantages of being aware of the degree to which Satan has invaded our churches? Is ignorance bliss?

5. What would you do about it if you found out it was a significant problem in your church?

Missive 11

Keep Them from the Book!

Nightcrawler:

You tell me that your latest "project" not only became a follower of the enemy but that he has shown an interest in reading the Book. How could you let things get so out of hand so quickly?

You could have distracted him while he was listening to the sermon. Didn't you notice that he was listening intently? You could have pointed out the pretty chick across the aisle or blown their public address system.

What a catastrophe! You have to work quickly—pull out all stops!

Do everything in your power to keep him away from the Book, as once he gets that into his head, it makes our job so much more difficult. You can distract him through fatigue, tantalizing sex, a demanding assignment at work. Use your imagination? Give his mother some dreadful illness! Have him get into a big fight with Rebecca, have his wife want him back or his son get deathly sick—think of something! Stupid! You must end his determination to read the Book, or we will have a big problem on our hands!

If all else fails and he is determined to read that awful work of the enemy, foster it being sporadic—when "the spirit moves." Devise things to interfere with any consistent reading. Remember, fatigue is on our side. If your project remembers at 10:00 p.m. that he hasn't read in the Book that day and is tempted to read his several chapters, or whatever—distract him. Remind him how hard a day he has had, the fact that he is tired and won't "get much out of it." He needs to get a good night's sleep as he has an important day tomorrow. Or maybe he'll read in the morning when he is fresh—anything to get him to put it off.

Above all don't let him get any of the enemy's ideas of having a reading plan—reading so many chapters a day and checking it off if he has read—or something like that. Once they get that far, it is much more difficult for us to sabotage their reading of the Book.

Your Unhappy,
Beelzebub

For Your Consideration

1. Honestly now, do you think Satan is concerned about your personal reading of the Book enough to try and *personally* interfere with it?

2. How big a deal is it to Satan that we don't read in the Book?

3. Describe the tactics Satan has used to keep you from reading the Book. What were the results? Have you discovered any techniques to combat Satan's attempt to keep you from God's word?

4. Let's say you have had a very busy time at work, putting in sixty or more hours a week, and have honestly been too tired to read the Book. Ideally how should one handle such times?

5. What do you think of the relationship now between Rebecca and Tom? Would you have any words of wisdom for Rebecca?

Missive 12

Reading in the Book!

Nightcrawler:

In our last correspondence I urged you to take immediate action and report back immediately. Since I didn't hear from you, I feared the worst—and unfortunately my fears were warranted. I looked in on your feeble attempts at dissuading your latest charge from reading the Book. Disgusting! Your puny attempt was utterly disgusting. He was so tired he could hardly keep his eyes open. You gave up after putting into his mind the thought one time: *You're tired; don't you think you should go to bed?*

Remember he gets horrible migraines. Have him think one is going to come on if he doesn't get enough sleep, or have his wife call his cell phone with concerns about his son's health. Have his boss call him and be upset about something he did at work that day. Think of something—stupid—anything to divert his attention.

And to think that he and Rebecca agreed they would check up on each other to see if they were reading—even if they didn't see each other that day. That is violation of rule number one—remember your basic training.

I have yet to decide how I will penalize you for your failure. But, you can be sure—it will come. Right now it is urgent that you quickly go to plan B—that is, direct them to portions that seem dull to new believers or parts that have to do with ancient laws that don't seem as apropos for today.

The portions that you want to avoid or at least decrease their exposure to are the gospels as they focus on the life and work of our greatest source of trouble. Next to be avoided are the epistles—they tell about the early working out of the enemy's message and the church.

If they are bound and determined to read the Book and you can't devise tactics to interfere—which seems to be the predicament you have gotten yourself into—then have them read it like any normal book: duh, from the beginning to the end. You will find the new inductees into his camp often bog down about the third or fourth book in, Leviticus and Numbers—they are godsends for us (pun intended)—and give up. Worst case scenario they will read through the Book from beginning to end. That way they will spend a lot of time on portions that are much harder to understand and may have less practical application. Don't misunderstand me—we want them to avoid the entire Book, but if that is not possible we can guide them—ha, ha!

One of your coworkers told me of one of his followers who was reading one chapter from the gospels every day in order to get the major exposure to our archenemy—one chapter in the rest of the New Testament, one chapter in the Psalms emphasizing praise to our enemy, and one chapter in the rest of the Old Testament. This is the very worst combination and exposure I could imagine— don't let such a preposterous idea get out of the bag. It emphasizes the very things we want the earthlings to avoid the most.

Your Very Unhappy Assessor,
Uncle Beelzebub

For Your Consideration

1. Do you think Rebecca should have terminated this relationship as soon as she found out he was married? If so what would have happened to Tom; or should that have been a concern for Rebecca? What is the risk with Rebecca continuing to see Tom?

2. How are you doing in reading the Book? Do you have any plan? Describe it.

3. Do some portions of Scripture warrant greater exposure than others? If so, which ones and why? What are you doing about it?

Missive 13

Tom's Concern for Others

My Very Fondest Uncle Beelzebub:

I got Tom's car to break down on the freeway, and this made him two hours late for work. Then I got his estranged wife to bawl him out for being five days late with his child support check. But even with all this, nothing seemed to deter Tom from his desire to read the Book.

But what alarmed me even more than that—he is talking to Rebecca about his concern for several colleagues at work who "don't know the L____!" You know who I mean.

I pulled out notes from our class and told him that we don't witness in this century; it was okay in previous centuries, but people wouldn't understand today. They would think you were an oddball or off your rocker! For good measure I added, "The boss might pass on your next raise or even fire you. You don't want them to think you are one of those J_____ freaks, do you?"

I have even tried to tempt Tom to have sex with Rebecca, thinking that that might get his spiritual interest off kilter, but nothing seemed to faze him. Help!

Your Very Affectionate and Appreciative,
Nightcrawler

For Your Consideration

1. Should you have a personal concern for the spiritual condition of those you rub shoulders with? Have you in the past? What has that looked like, or what do you think that should look like? What has been the outcome?

2. Do you pray for opportunities to share your faith? Is that important? What has been the result: in the past and more recently?

Missive 14

Blown!

Nightcrawler:

You have blown this one from beginning to end. If this were a football game, I would send you to the showers early—in our case to the ovens! Anyway, it's not our team that will send any of us to the ovens—it's *him*. So I guess I will have to stick with you for now—but be sure I am watching you very closely.

Since I didn't hear from you, I thought I would again check in on the earthlings under your charge. No wonder I haven't heard from you!

Tom is a lost cause, reading the Book regularly, went back to his wife, and taking her to church. He is also taking a real interest in his three-year-old. At work everyone has noticed a positive change in his life. A total lost cause.

Then I checked on Rebecca. She has felt good about the progress Tom is making but is being very careful not to get involved emotionally (you know what I mean) with him. However, she has felt totally lost, humanly speaking—missing the relationship with George but not knowing what do about that. She has thought about calling him—but was not sure that is the right thing to do.

Then George called her. It was a little strange. He said he would like to take her out for dinner but that he wanted her to drive her own car to their favorite restaurant. This seemed very odd, but she jumped at the chance. I didn't know what to think of it either!

They had a nice dinner together: small talk, catching up, etc. Then George said he would like to date—but it had to be different. He had been meeting regularly with a mature Christian fellow for accountability since they broke up. George went on to say that he had been addicted to pornography since fifteen and never was able to deal with it until the last couple of months when he found someone to meet with regularly and to be accountable to.

He wanted her to find a mature spiritual woman and meet on a regular basis so that both of them would be accountable for their dating and total spiritual life. He also wanted his accountability person to have permission to talk to her accountability person. That would make it a double check for both of them. When he said this, Rebecca broke down and bawled like a baby. This baffled George until she was able to gain her composure. She told him this is what she really wanted all along but was afraid guys, even nice Christian guys like him, would reject her for being a prude. Sure, she enjoyed sex but it also played havoc with her, especially spiritually. She readily agreed with his suggestion.

George said he would call her in two weeks and see if she had been able to start an accountability relationship with a mature Christian woman. Then they would take it from there.

Both were crying like babies as they kissed good-bye in the parking lot of their favorite restaurant.

Nightcrawler, this is just what we don't want to happen! It makes our job exceedingly difficult—virtually impossible! Try to tempt Rebecca to balk at this complicated accountability stuff—after all they are mature adults! They don't need an accountability partner! Keep close tabs on them, and keep me updated. I don't want any more slippage!

Your Most Very Unhappy,
Supervisor

For Your Consideration

1. How realistic is this missive? Explain your answer.

2. What do you think of each step in the interaction?

3. Both George and Rebecca are sincere Christians yet slipped into a sexual relationship. How common is this? What various options do they have to try to deal with their problem? How successful is each option likely to be?

4. Do you think accountability for pornography as a Christian is: a) optional, b) desirable, c) essential? Why? What about accountability for the temptation to engage in sex?

5. If a friend had a problem with pornography, how would you advise him or her to deal with it with a reasonable likelihood of success? How would you deal with one of these problems in your life?

6. Are our churches addressing these problems sufficiently? What would it look like if they did?

For personal consideration: If you have a problem in the sexual area, what would God have you do? You might consider writing a letter to Christ stating your plan to deal with the problem. Then you might share that with a close friend.

Missive 15

A Lost Cause

Nightcrawler:

I have noticed several more months have gone by since you wrote me about George and Rebecca, so again I thought I had better look in on them personally since you have failed to keep me updated. Have you even been checking up on them and trying to sabotage their movement toward our enemy?

No wonder you didn't report on them. They are a total loss! They are both seeing their accountability partner every couple of weeks. They are into the enemy's Book, counseling the young people's group, engaged again, and clean sexually. George slipped back once for several days to his favorite porn site, but that was quickly nipped in the bud the next time he got together with his accountability partner. What a total loss!

Then I checked on Tom. At first I was delighted as he called Rebecca and wanted some help. I thought what any of us from down below would think, *Yeah, sure he does; you know what he wants!*

He went to Rebecca's, and you could have blown me away. He didn't even touch her, and all excited, he said that Randy at work was interested in our enemy and what should he do now?

Rebecca carefully went through those, what were they called—I think they were Bill Bright's Four Spiritual Laws? First, that the Maker of the universe loves every last stinking human being and wants the very best for them. Can you fathom that? Second, that the very thing we encourage those earthlings to do—to rebel against, you know who—has separated that poor little earthling from G__ and the eternal splendor he has prepared for them throughout eternity. Third, that J_____, his Son, paid for their mistakes, also known by some as the s__ word, so that those horrible earthly creatures might spend eternity with him in splendor—while we bake in you know where. And fourth: that each and every last one of those earthlings must individually accept what he has done for them to experience what G__ has for them up in the skies, by and by. After she showed him those four spiritual laws, he said he felt ready to talk to Randy when the opportunity presented itself.

He then told Rebecca that he is taking his wife and son to church and they are talking about renewing their wedding vows—in church! Another total Loss! If that wasn't enough, one of his colleagues at work has noticed the change in Tom's life and has been reading daily from his grandmother's "old Book" ... you know the one I am talking about!

Nightcrawler, I would demote you if I could, but you are already at our lowest-ranking level. Doesn't that even motivate you to get your act together? If I were you, I would be trembling in my boots for the punishment our supreme leader, Satan, will heap on you when he hears about this.

Nightcrawler, it has been a long time, millennia, since I have gotten my hands dirty and dealt directly with those human scum bums, but you have done such a poor job I think I have no choice but to show you how it is done by an expert. So I will relieve you of your responsibility with Tom—but use the extra time to good advantage with your other charges.

Your Very Unhappy Supervisor,
B.

For Your Consideration

1. Does it surprise you that an accountability partner would make this much difference in Tom and Rebecca's lives? Discuss why this is the case.

2. Are there other options available if one is struggling with sexual temptations, and if so, what are they? What are their strengths and weaknesses?

3. Are you familiar with Bill Bright's "Four Spiritual Laws", as briefly described above, and what do you think of them?

4. Do you think that those that don't receive Christ's provision will spend eternity in hell? What might that hell be like?

5. Do you think this whole devil stuff and hell is a fantasy of religious nuts?

6. What is your reaction to this entire missive?

Missive 16

What's Next with Tom?

Uncle Beelzebub:

The other night I had a few free minutes and was curious as to how you were doing with Tom—since I had blown it with him—and wanted to learn from your expertise. Now I am more confused. When I looked in on him, his wife confessed she was having an affair with her boss, and Tom readily forgave her and admitted his own transgressions.

Their son was deathly sick with pneumonia, and, instead of him getting angry at God, he earnestly prayed, and it seemed to draw him closer to our enemy. There even may be permanent lung damage, but it didn't seem to alter his allegiance to our enemy. And the dimwit said to his wife that they would just have to rely on our enemy all the more.

Then he told his wife that the Book talks about hiding our enemy's word in their hearts, and because of this, he's memorizing a verse every week.

I know in the last century there were these religious nuts that memorized a lot from our enemy's Book. For young kids they had Awana Clubs that got their little rascals to memorize portions from the Book. Then there was that fanatical group called the

Gators—no, that's not right—they were called The Navigators. They had their little black packs, and they would go around mumbling verses to themselves. Fortunately, we squashed a lot of that. I know our boss sent up word that we should make sure nothing like that really gets going again! They were a real problem to us for a while.

Uncle, I'm really confused—is this the kind of results you want?

Your Understudy,
Nightcrawler

For Your Consideration

1. Do you know anyone who has become a believer in Christ and become zealous in his or her discipleship? Why do some become zealous in their pursuit of spiritual things and others plod along at best?

2. Have you memorized much of God's word? Are you doing it now? Do you think it is an optional undertaking or a must?

Missive 17

Mind Your Own Business

Nightcrawler:

Why are you wasting your time looking in on me instead of doing your own work? You don't have a second to waste looking in on my activities. You have got your hands full not to make more stupid mistakes like you have been making recently. You have already made too much work for me to bail you out of! Get to work, and let me handle Tom!

Your Very Unhappy Uncle,
B.

For Your Consideration

1. Why is Beelzebub irritated at Nightcrawler?

2. Review and explain the sequence of events that have taken place in the last several missives.

Missive 18

Spiking the Orange Juice with Birth Control Pills

Dear Uncle Beelzebub:

Before church I was observing Deacon Jones's home, and to my surprise I saw Mrs. Jones, secretively, open a bottle of birth control pills, grind one up, and put it in her fifteen-year-old-daughter's orange juice. I don't think the daughter or anyone else in the family had any idea the pill was in the orange juice when she drank it for breakfast.

Then, between Sunday school and church I noticed a heated discussion between Mrs. Jones, Mrs. Garcia, the choir director, and Mrs. Black, the pastor's wife. I was curious so I snuck over and listened in. It turns out that each of them has an adolescent daughter. They are all professing Christians—and "good girls." But each mother is concerned about the pressures on the young people today, especially in their community, and the possibility of a pregnancy. It turns out that Mrs. Jones discussed the entire issue with her daughter, and then they went to the doctor together and he prescribed a contraceptive. Mrs. Black was outraged when she heard that, saying, "Mind you, a Christian even considering such sinful action … that's murder!" But her twenty-one-year old has an illegitimate child living with her and her eighteen-year-old is seven months along, and Mrs. Black complains about them continually.

Mrs. Jones snorted: "Would you rather your daughter be an ill-prepared mother, drop out of school, go on welfare, have a son who at fifteen ends up on one end of a gun or the other, and at twenty is spending the rest of his life in jail?"

Mrs. Jones says she secretively puts a birth control pill in the orange juice as Deacon Jones would have a fit if he knew about it. Also, if her daughter knew, it might encourage her to have sex. This argument went on for twenty minutes! They even walked into church late, and their husbands gave them awful frowns.

Uncle Beelzebub, as you well know, this issue comes up often. What is our preferred position on this? I know you would encourage the pregnancies, as it perpetrates the plight many of these folks face—which we relish—unwanted early pregnancies, dropping out of school, poor parenting, juvenile delinquency, drugs, gangs, crime, jail, and more unwanted babies—especially in the impoverished communities. In undeveloped countries there is even more hunger. Should we encourage or discourage contraception?

Your Understudy,
Nightcrawler

For Your Consideration

1. Are all forms of birth control murder, sin?

2. If you had a fifteen-year-old that you knew was probably having sex and your only option was that he/she use some form of birth control or not to use any such control—which would you prefer? Why?

3. For society in general, what approach would you recommend if the choice were yours? Why? Would you make the same recommendation in the undeveloped world, where overpopulation and hunger prevail? What are the consequences of your choices?

Missive 19

Lesser of Two Evils?

Dear Nightcrawler:

I am glad you raised this question. As you know, many Christians have a very strong belief that any form of contraception is murder and therefore not only wrong, but **SIN**, spelled in bold, capital letters! Their Book does not actually say that, but for them it is:

The Eleventh Commandment: *Any form of contraception is sin!*

We actually are not sure if this is how the enemy himself feels, but our council's conclusion is that this notion works to our best advantage. As an aside, our studies have revealed that most of his followers in the developed world have used some form of birth control—many of the same ones—including their leaders that speak so adamantly against it! In fact we did a little study and found that 62 percent of married Christian leaders that preach against using contraception have at some point in their lifes used contraception! Can you believe that! You can usually spot them pretty fast. Any couple that has been married for twenty years or more between the ages of fifteen and fifty-five who have four or fewer children have probably used contraceptives.

At any rate, our studies have also shown that, in general, worldwide, individuals who have unwanted pregnancies are more likely to have kids who drop out or never go to school, get in trouble with the law, use drugs, misuse guns, and end up in jail. That is a high five for us. So our Supreme Council, with the support of Satan himself, has ruled unanimously that any form of birth control is to be discouraged among the poor. That's right— you heard me right—we agree on this one with the Fundies— especially for the unmarried and in parts of the world where poverty, crime, and hunger are prevalent.

We don't really know what our archenemy thinks about this, but we sure know what his followers think he thinks!

Your Affectionate,
Uncle Beelzebub

For Your Consideration

1. The statistics quoted in *this* missive are the scribe's estimations. What would your estimate be on each of these issues?

2. How do you feel about the United States paying for contraception in poor countries where the population rate is high and hunger is a problem? How do you feel about the United States putting pressure on poor countries to foster birth control?

3. Should "lesser of two evils" ever be in a Christian's vocabulary? Explain your answer. Discuss the advantage and disadvantage of your view and that of those who would see it differently.

4. Can you think of any scripture that might support the principle of permissive will or "lesser of two evils" but doesn't use those exact words? Does a passage like Matthew 19:8 shed any possible light? This is the passage where the Pharisees came to Christ asking about divorce. Christ responded that God permitted it "Because of your hardness of heart …". Are there any other examples that might fall into the category of "God's permissive will," and what are the possible consequences if we take what might be considered God's second best?

Missive 20

Padding the Expense Account and Cheating on Taxes

Dear Uncle Beelzebub:

Recently I was assigned John. He has his own contracting business building and remodeling homes. He came from the "wrong side of the tracks" but is upwardly mobile and his wife likes "nice things." He is active at church and professes to be a "Christian contractor," advertises as such, and is quite visible at church … but his spiritual depth is paper thin. He is prone to use inferior material in his building and pads his mileage and expenses accounts. His business is in his name, and if someone just puts his name on the check, he has been known to "by mistake" deposit it into his personal checking account instead of the business account. He keeps a record of what he gives to the "Lord's work," but even that seems inflated.

Uncle, Andy is clearly dishonest, but everyone thinks he is a wonderful, honest, dedicated Christian. So, Uncle, what should my approach be:

1) Have someone sue him for misrepresentation or faulty workmanship;

2) Have the IRS find out his deception and go after him; or

3) Just encourage his double life and let him get away with it until, you know who, takes care of him at the judgment seat?

Your Understudy,
Nightcrawler

For Your Consideration

1. What approach do you think Satan would prefer and why?

2. What are the advantages and disadvantages as far as Satan is concerned with each approach?

3. Why don't you try your hand at writing your own "Nightcrawler's Missives" and share them with those you are discussing these missives with?

Missive 21

Which is Preferable: Judgment Now or Later?

Nightcrawler:

I am glad you raised this question. Satan's preferred handling of a situation depends on several factors. If the individual is a well-recognized big shot and associated with our enemy, then Satan's preferred outcome is a giant scandal that makes news—the bigger the news the better. You know the kind we like—like the well-known, very conservative, give them hellfire and brimstone TV pastor. Our boss enjoys a good laugh after one of these guys fall. It also gives the "world" a lot of ammunition to make fun of Christians!

On the other hand if the subject is "small potatoes"—that is, it wouldn't even make the local papers—then Satan would rather he or she keep getting away with it. There are several reasons for this. First, their actions and ability to get away with it might influence others to follow suit. Second, he or she will feel smug; think he or she is really pulling the wool over someone's eyes. As time passes, these people will become immune to what they are doing, thinking it is "normal," "not so bad," "everybody is doing it." Satan is very content to have them think they are getting away with it as long as they live—that is, live on this earth. Then they will have the surprise of their lives in the world to come—we will have company in the most intense part of you know where. Furthermore, their shady Christian life will be a poor testimony for all those that do business with them.

So remember, Nightcrawler: Satan's rule is for earthlings to get away with as much as they can while on earth. The fewer the consequences, the better; the more inconsistent the consequences are, the better. That way we will have a lot more company later on. Got it? *Good*!

Look at it this way. If he gets caught early, he is more likely to learn from his misdeeds, also known by the enemy as s__, and repent. Satan's preference is to let him get away with it throughout his earthly life. As the years pass, he will think what he is doing is perfectly normal. Furthermore, his shady business practices, as a professing follower of our enemy, will turn off many from following our enemy.

Your Affectionate,
Uncle Beelzebub

For Your Consideration

1. Discuss the pros and cons of getting caught now or only in eternity?

2. If you were writing this missive, would you draw the same conclusion as the scribe does? If not, how would you write this missive?

Missive 22

Alphabet Soup

Dear Nightcrawler:

Satan himself had a royal banquet last night for all of us upper-echelon officers of his army. Sorry there wasn't enough room for you. In any case, we needed to keep most of you lower-level staff working the streets. Can't let up for a minute, you know.

Most earthlings picture Satan in a red suit with a pitchfork—a total misrepresentation—but let's keep it that way; it's to our advantage. It helps perpetuate the fairytale—like quality associated with all of us and our work. Anyway, Satan was dressed in a three-piece suit, red hair, colorful tie, and all. He reminded me a lot of some narcissistic politicians I know. They have big egos, and it's all about them!

By the end of the evening, we were feeling pretty high, laughing at all the past successes and thinking about opportunities the future holds. The coup de grace was the University of California asking the enrollees on their college entrance applications their sex and giving not only the opportunities to check "Male" and "Female" but also "Lesbian," "Gay," "Bisexual," "Transgender," and "Other."[9] They are also going to be adding more choices to their bathrooms. Our aim is like their book says for every man, ah … that is … person, to do what is right in his'/hers'/its'/theirs'/ or whatevers' own eyes.

Satan unveiled his ten-year plan. He said originally it was his hundred-year plan, but they have had so many successes that he hopes in ten years to have his/her/it/their, or whatevers in every high school and most of the grammar schools. Won't that be a blast! Think of the poor, confused five-year-old looking at the doors and wondering which he, no she, no it, should go into today. Then watch the bullies have a field day as it comes out!

In addition, Satan is pushing to require, by law, all public establishments to have bathroom accommodations for "Other" and then to see what churches will do to meet those requirements. Nightcrawler, there are fun times ahead until it all abruptly ends—but I don't even want to go there! I am going to enjoy it as long as I can and take as many earthlings with me as I can! As you well know, misery loves company, and we are going to have a lot of both!

Your Very Happy,
Uncle Beelzebub

For Your Consideration

1. How do you think a Christian should respond to the sexual revolution inroads?

2. Picture Christ walking on the earth today, and describe how you think he might respond to the sexual revolution.

Missive 23

Supreme Court and "Gay Rights"

My Dear Nightcrawler:

President Obama applauded the decision to make same-sex marriages the law of the land and even celebrated with rainbow-colored lights adorning the White House on June 26, 2015. Some are saying the White House lost its lily white purity that dark night.

Lucifer himself broke out the champagne, struck up the band, and had rainbow-colored lights flashing in the dungeon that night. It was not so much for the decision itself but for the future opportunities it will give all of us. There is no end to the possibilities this opens up. One fun game plan is to have our agents find individuals dedicated to the enemy, such as owners of bakeries, and order cakes saying, "God bless this wedding" and see what they do. That should be such fun; I can't wait to see them squirm! But activities like this will be peanuts compared to the bigger issues in our strategy book. The time will come when organizations that don't embrace LGBTs as fully-fledged members and leaders of their organization will lose their tax exempt status—first in parachurch organizations and then in churches themselves! It's impossible to imagine what this crack in the door will let in—in our future. Let your imagination run wild, Nightcrawler—fun's a comin'! We might even get some organizations outlawed and many of his followers in the clinker over this one.

The chief justice warns that the wording allows believers to "advocate" for their faith but leaves open to question if they can practice their religion. How about that—a country established on the basis of being able to practice their faith soon putting in jail someone for honestly practicing his or her faith. You haven't seen the beginning yet! Don't tell anyone, but that sounds like grand liberty for us and no justice for them—goodie! I can't wait!

Your Cordial Assessor,
Uncle Beelzebub

For Your Consideration

1. Should a president celebrate a decision like applauding same-sex marriages? Would you feel the same way if the Supreme Court had voted it down and the president celebrated that decision?

2. What ultimate effects will the Supreme Court decision have on society, and how do you think God would have his followers respond? Would you be willing to go to jail over this issue? Does it rise to that level for anyone?

Missive 24

Go to Jail to Get a Free $25,000 Sex-Reassignment Surgery

Dear Nightcrawler:

I must commend you even though I thought you had gone off your rocker for even trying to get the state of California to pay for sex-reassignment surgery for criminals in jail. These are individuals whom our enemy made males, but they didn't like that they weren't consulted ahead of time in that arbitrary assignment and now want to become females. So you arranged for two so-called learned mental health experts to determine that these two males who had committed very significant crimes against society, including murder, were suffering from "dysphoria" and should get a $25,000 sex-reassignment surgery paid for by law-abiding citizens.

Dysphoria means an emotional state characterized by anxiety, depression, unease, and comes from the Greek word "distress" or "hard to bear." Some might even distort this and think that is what jail is all about.

California alone has about four hundred transgender inmates already receiving sex-altering medications, and surgery on them would cost about ten billion law-abiding dollars.

Medicare and all insurance policies are already required to pay for sex-reassignment surgery, and guess who is paying for that?[10] I wonder if that is what his book means about every whatever doing what is right in their own eyes.

You know, while you are at it, I would suspect prison conditions in general are a little dysphoric, so Nightcrawler, have you thought about pushing for five-star hotel quarters to house all the prisoners? Anything less, I would think, would be criminal! It might cause some uncomfortable feelings, and you can't let that happen, of all places, in jail! I hope they are getting plenty of feel-good drugs like Xanax, Valium, Ativan, and the like. While they are at it, I suspect a few criminals are a little dysphoric over baggy eyelids, so let's get them to throw in a facelift while we are at it—after all, the taxpayers won't know the difference!

Your Very Happy Overseer and Advisor,
Uncle Beelzebub

For Your Consideration

1. Do you think we should be using tax dollars to pay for such things as sex-reassignment surgery at $25,000 each for prisoners who feel uncomfortable in their God-assigned sexual role?

2. There have been jails that have been cruel in the past, and some may exist in the free world currently; however, do you think some have gone too far in the other direction in recent years?

Missive 25

Prayer for Our Leaders

Dear Nightcrawler:

A few years ago someone got the idea in the so-called United States to set aside a day to pray for the country and its leaders. This even got Lucifer's attention, and we pulled out all stops to prevent it. But you know—the National Day of Prayer hasn't amounted to that much of a threat. There certainly are some who do take it very seriously, but for most it's kind of a perfunctory thing—and at most it lasts only one day. All the rest of the year it is rare for them to pray for their leaders in private or public. The few who do pray for their leaders keep it pretty generic.

Their manual tells them to pray for those in authority. Nightcrawler, very rarely an understudy reports that in a so-called evangelical church they prayed for those in authority, especially if it is a leader they didn't vote for! It would seem to me that those they didn't vote for need as much, if not more, prayer than those they voted for. Once or maybe twice an understudy has reported they have prayed for "O'-ba'-ma" but said in kind of a derogative tone; never "Our President, Mr. Obama" or at least just plain "Mr. Obama," something like that—that shows at least a measure of respect. What a delightful, "devilish" putdown! Good work! No … that is really great work!

One of our understudies recently took it upon himself to do a little survey of one hundred conservative, so-called evangelical churches—clearly in the enemy's camp—and not one of them had prayed specifically for the president by name on the Sunday evaluated. Six of them prayed generically for "our leaders"—that's a whopping 6 percent. The so-called liberals do a better job of this than the so-called conservatives. But we don't lose as much sleep over the effectiveness of their prayers! (Note: I slipped into using earthling slang as—of course—none of our team needs to sleep—we are active 24/7 to use another of their terms.)

Their personal prayer life is even more revealing. Another of our understudies listened in on one hundred of his followers, and on the day evaluated he found only two individuals prayed for the country's leaders. I think—no, I know—we are winning that battle, and it shows in the decisions the leaders make.

Your Cordial Assessor,
Uncle Beelzebub

For Your Consideration

1. At your church, how often do they pray for the president? Should we pray for other leaders, such as congress, our military leaders, the Supreme Court, and the state government?

2. When our leaders make bad decisions, to what extent do we bear responsibility if we haven't prayed for them and their decisions?

3. Should we pray for wisdom for those we didn't vote for as well as for those we did? Or do we want them to fail even if it adversely affects our country? How do you pray for those in office you don't like? How would God have you pray for them?

4. The statistics quoted in this missive are totally a guess by the scribe. What would your guess be for the statistics cited?

5. Will there be more prayer for a President Trump than a President Obama?

6. What criteria should we use in praying for our leaders?

Missive 26

Why Do Earthlings Go to Church?

My Dear Uncle Beelzebub:

You're more knowledgeable than I with a much higher rank than I have—help me understand something: Why do earthling followers of our enemy go to church anyway?

On Sunday morning it is one mad rush. First there is a fight over how long fifteen-year-old Janet spent in the bathroom. They're all rushing. It's worse than when they have to go to school and work. There invariably is an argument on the way to church. Why the seventeen-year-old wasn't ready on time—they're going to be late. Do they have to go to the in-laws for lunch again?

But then magic occurs. The moment they arrive at church and open the car door and greet the Smiths, they are all one big, happy, smiling family!

On the way home from church, it seems like they come away more judgmental and critical than when they enter the sanctuary—and that's nothing to brag about!

Sometimes I will ride home with them or sit with them at their Sunday lunch, and it seems like it is an opportunity to have the pastor for lunch. They discuss what they did or didn't like about the music, how the announcements were given, and what the choir sang. For the main course they dissect Pastor Anderson's message. It was too long or too short, and his jokes were corny this morning! After they have roasted him, they move on to dress! Did you notice the choir director's low-cut blouse—"and in church!" Why didn't Mrs. Murphy take her crying baby out sooner? Didn't she realize how annoyed everyone was? Everyone was looking her way for ten minutes. And so it goes Sunday after Sunday—of course with minor variations.

Then to top it all off, they conclude with the statement that they "didn't get much out of the sermon" today! What do they expect!

So, Uncle, why do earthling followers of our enemy go to church? When I listen to their conversation before and after church, I don't have the foggiest idea why they go. Why do they go to church? Tell me what their motive is so I can sabotage it. Or should I just leave well enough alone—it is fine the way it is?

Your Understudy,
Nightcrawler

For Your Consideration

1. What parts of this missive are true to your personal experience? What can you not identify with?

2. How often are you critical about church, the congregants, the message, or the pastor?

3. In your heart of hearts, why do *you* really go to church? Elaborate.

4. Should we go to church to worship God or "to get something out of it"? Explain the different mind-set and the likely result.

5. What should our motive be when we go to church?

6. What would characterize your ride to and from church? Do you ever have the pastor or church for lunch?

Missive 27

God Only Knows Why They Go to Church

My Dear Nightcrawler:

You asked why earthlings go to church. You know that would make an interesting survey! For most of them I think it is just part of their weekly ritual—"it is what we have always done on Sunday." It is sort of like washing your face in the morning.

I don't think that most of them know why. Oh yes, if you asked, they would give some reasonable answers. "God commands it. I need it to worship or to function the following week. The kids need the spiritual training," or something along that line. But in reality they are just going through the motions—like washing dishes after dinner! And there is no more heart preparation for worship than to wash the dishes.

Nightcrawler—I don't think you need to do a thing to sabotage church. I think they do it for us! Just sit back and enjoy the ride next time you observe their Sunday ritual!

Your Affectionate,
Uncle Beelzebub

For Your Consideration

1. Do you do anything to enrich your worship experience or to sabotage it?

2. Do you need to do any preparation before you go to church? If so, what might it be? Do your expectations make any difference? What kind of an example are you modeling for your family or others?

Missive 28

Judgmental Deacon

My Dear Uncle Beelzebub,

Last Sunday morning I watched with amusement as Deacon Anderson walked into the 11:00 a.m. service in his church and in front of him sat a teenager who was really getting into the worship, clapping his hands when they weren't raised, and flapping around blocking Deacon Anderson's view. The youth wore flip-flops, cutoffs, a tank top, and to top it all off a baseball hat turned backward. This inconsiderate youngster totally destroyed the deacon's worship that morning. One could see the deacon preoccupied and seething with this inconsiderate youth. And when they filed out of church, the ill-dressed youngster gave Deacon Anderson a big smile and nodded his head. All Deacon Anderson could muster up was an indiscernible growl and frown of disapproval. He later told Mrs. Anderson that he hoped his frown was observed and the inconsiderate youth got the message that his behavior was totally unacceptable in God's house.

After church I heard the teenager tell his live-in girlfriend how much he had gotten out of the service and that he might have returned next Sunday—that is, until that self-righteous man all dressed up in a suit, white shirt, tie, and fluffy gray hair looked at him with judgmental disapproval—and now he wasn't so sure he would ever go to church again!

Uncle Beelzebub, I think I got two for zero—it made my day. I didn't do anything, and they both destroyed each other's worship of the enemy. That's cool—and you know, we've got to get all the cool moments while we can … I don't like to think about the day when there will be no more cool moments—only heat! So I am going to bask in the enemy's beautiful weather while I still can!

On another subject, earthlings come to church, some dressed in suits and ties, others in tank tops; some women dress like they are going to the beach and others like they were going to the Oscars. What should we encourage?

Your Understudy,
Nightcrawler

For Your Consideration

1. What in *your* church might encourage or discourage a younger visitor to return? What about an older visitor?

2. How much does our dress and conduct affect the likelihood that visitors will return for future visits? What are visitors prone to notice? Should we be concerned about what other people, including visitors, think about how we dress?

3. Does it make any difference how we dress when we go to church? Does it make any difference to God?

Missive 29

Dress and Worship in Church

My Dear Nightcrawler:

You know Nightcrawler, personally, I could not care less what earthlings wear in church, but what I would like to know is what our mortal enemy—no, no, that's not the right word—our eternal enemy wants earthlings to wear and then encourage the opposite. In olden times Moses was told to take off his shoes as he was on holy ground. When priests went into the Holy of Holies, they went with a rope tied around their foot to pull them out if they didn't meet God's standards, and he struck them dead on the spot. If that rule applied today, I bet we would have a stinking mess in every church! Maybe that is why the rule no longer exists!

The synagogue seemed to be a pretty sophisticated and sterile place. They had to wash properly before they worshiped, and there was a separate place for men and women to worship. But what blew my mind was that when C_____ came to earth in his physical form, he didn't seem to care much about all that ritual. He criticized the religious leaders of the day for washing on the outside and being filthy on the inside. It's funny, God gives all these strict laws in the Old Testament and then C_____ comes along and puts a new spin on them. Help me understand that, will you? The New Testament house churches were pretty informal. I can't remember how much we got involved with the Catholics putting on the robes and burning incense and the like—I think they conjured that up on their own. It made it seem more holy—sanctified!

Maybe God doesn't give a hoot about dress (as long as one is modestly adorned), and one can worship in tank tops and flip-flops as well as suits and ties. Maybe, just maybe it is true: "man looks at the outward appearance and God looks at the heart." Now that would be something! But don't let the earthlings comprehend that. We want to keep the focus on the external stuff—it allows earthlings more things to be judgmental about, and most importantly it keeps them from focusing on him—you know who I mean!

On the other hand, if an earthling was invited to the White House for dinner, I don't think they would have a big discussion on how to dress. I don't think there would be many tank tops, baseball caps, or flip-flops! It is a sign of respect to dress nicely!

Maybe what really counts is that earthlings are making melody and adoration from their hearts to God, whether it's with drums in Africa or the United States, guitars in South America, or a full orchestra in Carnegie Hall.

Your Affectionate,
Uncle Beelzebub

For Your Consideration

1. Some older people remember with fondness everyone dressing up in their best clothes on Sunday. Men came in suits and ties, women in nice modest clothes, and children wearing their best outfits. It feels to them that something has been lost in the last few decades—maybe a certain reverence. How do you respond to their feelings? Is there any validity in how they feel? Should that have any bearing on the dress of others?

2. If we dressed up to go to the White House, should we do any less to go into God's house?

3. If you were invited to the White House, how would you dress? Should that be any consideration when we think about appropriate dress to go into God's house? On the other hand, Christ seemed to invite all to come to him as they were—should that be a model?

4. If someone comes to church sloppily dressed, does this reflect on God or their attitude toward God?

5. Do you have any expectations about how people dress if you invite them over for dinner?

6. Where does "Man looks on the outward appearance, God looks on the heart" fit in—or does it in this situation?

7. Really, does it make any difference to God how people dress to go to church? To man? Should it?

Missive 30

A Gay Couple Visits a Conservative Evangelical Church

My Dear Uncle Beelzebub,

Two of my charges are Bill and Bob, a gay couple who grew up in one of our enemy's strongest churches. During adolescence they both discovered they were gay and came out—and of course their church rejected them. Now they are in their forties and live in another town. Last week they were lying in bed talking about how they missed something they used to have in church, so they decided to visit the church at Fifth and Broadway next Sunday.

The following Sunday Bill and Bob drove up to Conservative Evangelical Church, parked in the church's parking lot, got out, and walked up to the church holding hands. Reactions were interesting. Parishioners watched, and conversations stopped mid-sentence. Some looked at the couple as if a bag lady was approaching and moved aside, giving more room, and then turned away. One mother abruptly pulled her five-year-old son's arm as she changed direction to avoid the couple. Friendly George went out of his way to be warm and cordial, but his nervousness showed through.

As Bill and Bob went up the church steps, the head usher was awkwardly friendly. As the couple got their worship folders and walked down the center aisle, the song leader stopped mid sentence as he was announcing the next song, and most of the congregation turned and looked at the couple finding their seats down front. When late comers came into the sanctuary, they seemed to avoid sitting near Bob and Bill. Throughout the service it seemed like they were being watched closely out of the corner of people's eyes.

Bill and Bob's exit from church was similar to their entrance. A luncheon was advertised in the church worship folder immediately following the service in the church basement, but no one invited them to it.

They drove down Main Street and had lunch at the local bar, where they felt welcome and at home, stating church wasn't for them anymore!

Dear Uncle, I didn't have to do anything. The evangelicals solved what I worried might be a big problem for me.

Have a nice Sunday night. I would say a day of rest, but of course, we of the underworld don't get any days of rest, especially on Sundays—it's the busiest and most productive day of our week!

Your Understudy,
Nightcrawler

For Your Consideration

1. What is your reaction to this missive?

2. Try to imagine and then discuss how Bill and Bob would be treated in *your* church were they to attend next Sunday.

3. How do you believe God would have you and your church respond to Bill and Bob—or is this important to God?

4. Would some education be appropriate in your church or other Christian groups as to how Christ would have you relate to an LGBT individual?

Missive 31

Music in the Church

My Dear Nightcrawler:

Some time ago you asked about music in the church, which brings up an important issue that Satan's key generals have been trying to figure out in recent years, especially since the so-called hippie movement of the 1970s. If we can figure out what the enemy wants, then we can encourage what he dislikes. Make sense?

When the reprobate Luther started plagiarizing bar tunes and putting religious words to them, we were sure the enemy would disapprove, so we encouraged such music. But how wrong we were! Before we knew it hymns praising G__ were being sung across the nations and even in Carnegie Hall. Eventually most people didn't know the melodies were bar tunes. We sure messed up on that one—so that's all the more reason we need to get it right this time!

When the hippies came to church in the 70s, they brought their guitars, drums, and flip-flops. That sure upset the traditionalists—and often still does. But they're here to stay.

Therefore, Satan's chief council has decided since both forms of music are pretty well accepted in worship and, when sung from the heart, are valued by our enemy. So it seems the best way to proceed is to have each group be critical of the other. Just maybe we can split churches up over this! If possible, we can get one group to force their music on the other group.

It seems like just yesterday when King David was dancing in the streets of Jerusalem to God and David's better-than-thou wife threw a temper tantrum in disgust. She paid a handsome price for that! No more chamber time with the king! Earthling rule number one ought to be, "You don't criticize the king, especially if he is your own husband!" In fact it is risky to criticize your husband even if he is not king—and thinks he is! King David kept his distance from her after that; but of course, he had plenty of other wives and mistresses to take her place. He'd never get away with that today!

Maybe what is important is that people make a joyful noise from the heart unto our enemy, and that can take many forms. But those earthlings tend to be parochial—their way or the highway! "That's the way we have always done it!" Let's keep fostering that heart attitude—that fosters selfishness—and for goodness' sake—no that's not right—for badness' sake, that's what we want.

Your Cordial Assessor,
Uncle Beelzebub

For Your Consideration

1. Is music a problem in your church? If it is, how have you tried to solve the problem of different preferences? Is it reasonably satisfactory to all parties?

2. Relative to music, what matters to God? How important is it to consider "what we like"? What others like? Do you think God has any preference in these issues? If so, what?

3. From God's point of view, which is more important, the music or of the heart attitude?

Missive 32

What Ever Happened to Sin?

Dear Nightcrawler:

I just want to remind you how far we have come since our archenemy created the beautiful garden for Adam and Eve. I won't bore you with the millennia of ups and downs of our enticing humans to sin. It is well documented in the secular record and in the enemy's Book.

But the 1960s and '70s stand out to me—we were making phenomenal progress desensitizing humans to sin. I think the big breakthrough came when we were able to get the church to accept divorce. God gave us a wonderful gift when he gave humans sex. And my how we continue to use it to our advantage!

In 1973 Karl Menninger, a psychiatrist, of all people, wrote a book that became a sensation. Its title was, *Whatever Became of Sin?* Kenneth Woodward picked up on this in a cover article in *Newsweek* titled "What Ever Happened to Sin?" He stated:

> In earlier eras, ministers regularly exhorted congregations to humbly "confess our sins." But the aging baby boomers who are rushing back to church do not want to hear sermons that might rattle their self-esteem. And many

clergy, who are competing in a buyer's market, feel they cannot afford to alienate. To be sure, liberal ministers—and many a rabbi—routinely condemn such "systemic" social evils as racism, sexism and other updated permutations of the Mosaic Ten Commandments. But their voices are strangely muffled on subjects close to home—like divorce, pride, greed and overwhelming personal ambition. Fundamentalist preachers still excoriate abortion, pornography and other excesses of an anything-goes society. But these jeremiads are fists shaken at the world outside, not fingers pointed at those in the pews.[11]

With Menninger and Woodward and all the publicity at the time, I thought we were doomed—you know what I mean. However, it was only a blip. The church and the developed world have continued its downhill slide. Sin does that! We were able to start this slide in Europe, but the United States is not far behind.

What is so remarkable is that God has often used external enemies to try to jar his people to see the sinfulness of their ways and to repent. But they often were—and remain tone deaf to God's appeal. They focus on the external enemy and fail to see that the enemy is within and it is called sin. Today the West is worried and focusing on the Jihadists; they fail to see that the real enemy is within and God is using the Jihadists to get their attention before it is too late. What is that passage from that most dreaded book: "If my people, which are called by my name, shall humble themselves, and pray, and seek my face, and turn from their wicked ways; then will I hear from heaven, and will forgive their sin, and will heal their land."[12]

It's a good thing Billy Graham is in his waning years; otherwise he would he wagging his finger at stadiums full of people, telling them they need to repent lest America destroy itself or the Almighty allows the Jihadists to do it for him.

Nightcrawler, don't let the free world focus for a moment on the fact that they might be a big part of the current problem; keep the focus on the damn Jihadists and encourage the "free world" in its self-centered pursuit of sin and condemnation of all Muslims.

Your Giddy Supervisor,
Uncle Beelzebub

For Your Consideration

1. The scribe of this letter seems to be saying that our sin, America's sin, the free world's sin, is the cause or at least a major reason for Jihadists' attacks on Christians and the free world. Is this a fair assessment? Discus your rationale.

2. Other than in a song or creed being read, when is the last time you heard sin discussed in church?

3. In decades and centuries past, individuals were beat up with accusations about their sins and trespasses. Do you think that is what the scribe is advocating? How should this issue be handled in your church, in society? In your life?

4. Those of you who are older, do you view any particular time when the consciousness of sin seemed to be lost in the church, society, or your life? To those under forty: what does the concept of sin mean? Describe.

5. Is it possible to have an excessive preoccupation with sin? What might that look like, and what are its consequences?

6. What would a balanced approach look like?

Missive 33

Preaching on Heaven and Hell!

Dear Uncle Beelzebub:

I have a question for you. Last night I noticed the human scribe who has hacked into our communications talking to a friend on the phone, and I thought I would spy on him—so I listened in. I figured he must be in his early eighties! He has never attended seminary or even Bible school, but during his lifetime he estimates he has heard between four thousand and five thousand sermons or religious lectures of at least twenty minutes but many up to fifty minutes in length. He goes on to say that he has heard thousands of references to heaven and hell, but he has never heard one complete sermon on heaven or hell—period![13] He believes there ought to be one sermon of at least fifteen minutes in length, but preferably longer, on heaven every five years in every church. He also believes that there should be at least one sermon on hell of at least ten minutes at least every ten years in every church.

That sounds alarming to me. I would think we ought to squash this idea right away.

Uncle, what do you think?

Awaiting Your Learned Answer,
Nightcrawler

For Your Consideration

1. How many complete sermons have you heard on heaven? On hell?

2. What are the consequences of preaching on these subjects too much? Too little?

3. What do you think of the scribe's suggestion?

Missive 34

Response to Preaching on Heaven and Hell!

Dear Nightcrawler:

I am flattered that you would want to know my opinion on preaching on heaven and hell. I tried to tell Satan himself my learned opinion on this, but he has so much pride he didn't want to hear anything from anyone under him—the epitome of self-centeredness!

Since you asked me: my first choice would be for earthlings not to go to any religious kinds of services and view life as consisting of seventy or so years and then it's all over. Like an animal you return to dust—there is nothing more. Thus there is no need to even talk about an afterlife—there is none! That will encourage people to live like … ah … the devil himself and go to you know where with him—and us!

My second choice would be to let earthlings go to a pseudo-religious service, a "do-good" kind of fairly large gathering promoting some "do-good" program and give the attendees a sort of vague, "We all go back to earth where we came from" or if that doesn't work then, "We'll all go to some sort of better place by and by."

It's hard to know where to go from here. If they must preach more about eternity, then I guess I would have them touch on it in passing but so lightly that if the person yawned in church they would miss it.

Or on the other hand, my third choice would have them go to the opposite extreme. A harsh fire and brimstone preaching—you know the kind of a hundred years ago—would be my next choice. Hopefully that will scare them right out of … ah, church! But skip the heaven bit.

Above all else, do not talk about the person having any responsibility in where they will spend eternity—none, period!

Well, Nightcrawler, that's my best take on what Lucifer would want and what our enemy would not want.

Thanks for seeking my expert advice on this issue. It is flattering, which as you know is always appreciated!

Your Grateful, Knowledgeable,
Uncle Beelzebub

For Your Consideration

1. What do you think of Beelzebub's recommendations?

2. Do you even think there is an afterlife?

3. How much preaching on heaven and hell do you think is ideal?

Missive 35

Beelzebub, I'm Afraid!

My Dear Uncle Beelzebub:

Uncle, when I look at all the progress that we have made for so many millennia and now how things are shaping up in the Middle East, I know our time is short. I try not to think about it—but in my quiet moments, it resurfaces. I know you would tell me to work harder and get my mind off such negative stuff—quit thinking about myself. Most of the time I am successful in doing that, but now and then it creeps back into my thoughts.

Humans don't realize how fortunate they are—as long as they are alive and our enemy hasn't returned to call things quits, they can get right with their Creator and spend eternity in that beautiful place we were kicked out of long ago—all because of our sin. If only they knew how fantastic it is!

We blew it so many millennia ago when we all rebelled and our exile was permanent, irreversible—period. Ever since then we have been working our tails off—so to speak. If we are going to "you know where"—we want as much company as possible.

Uncle, some nights I have this recurring image of all humankind walking toward this giant cliff, unaware of what is ahead for them. Some will be going to eternal splendor with their

God. Many, as many as we can cajole to join us, are plunging into the depths below to gather with us one day for eternity. Sometimes I even feel sorry for them. Am I too sentimental?

Awaiting Your Answer,
Nightcrawler

For Your Consideration

1. This missive suggests that someday the world as we know it will come to an end and individuals will face an eternity in God's splendor or in a place of punishment with the angelic beings that rebelled against God before the world, as we know it, began. What do you think of this notion? If this is, in fact, true, do you know how you could avoid Beelzebub's and Nightcrawler's fate? Describe how you would respond if someone approached you and wondered how they could be assured of going to heaven.

2. What is your reaction to all of these missives? Does this technique of writing and questions serve any useful function? If so, describe. Are they harmful? Is the sarcasm and a few personal references appropriate or inappropriate?

3. If you were writing these missives, would you change them in any way? If so, how?

4. Are there some missives that you would add? If so, describe.

5. Do you think reading these missives and going through the questions will eternally change your life in any way? If so, describe. If not, do you think your loving heavenly Father would have your life altered in any way?

6. Do you think of anyone who might benefit from reading these missives? Would it be appropriate for you to give them a copy?

What Beelzebub Doesn't Want You to Know[14]

One thing that Nightcrawler had right is that all humankind is moving toward a giant, so to speak, cliff, unaware of what is ahead of them. Some will be going to eternal splendor with God. Many others, as many as the evil, Satanic forces can cajole, will join them to spend *eternity* in a *physical, conscious, painful state*—the exact nature of which is not fully revealed. But the description in the Bible is one of the most awful places that you could imagine, a place that you would not want to spend a minute—to say nothing of an unending period of time— eternity. Christ came to redeem you from that. You cannot earn that redemption, but you can accept it as a gift. Briefly the steps are as follows.

First, the Bible clearly teaches that God loves and cares for each one of us, and that includes *you*. God says, "I have loved you with an everlasting love: Therefore I draw you with lovingkindness."[15] He is also interested in every aspect of our lives—physical, mental, and spiritual. He has a plan for our lives and desires that we each experience an abundant and fulfilled life with personal peace—a life that ultimately only he can give. This is why Christ came to earth some two thousand years ago, that we "might have life, and might have it abundantly."[16]

Second, the Bible states that we are all basically self-centered individuals pursuing our own thing to the exclusion of God and thereby sinning against him. In the Old Testament we are depicted as sheep who have wandered away from the shepherd: "All we like sheep have gone astray; Each of us has turned to his own way."[17] It is this self-centeredness that keeps us at odds with God and His plan for our life. Our refusal to acknowledge our condition can keep us from ever understanding God's will for us. "There is none righteous, not even one; There is none who understands, There is none who seeks for God; All have turned aside, together they have become useless; There is none who does good. There is not even one."[18] When we insist that we have not sinned against God, we are rejecting his clear diagnosis and cannot make use of his prescription.

Third, Jesus Christ is God's gift and only remedy for our sin. The Bible states regarding Christ's death and resurrection that "Christ also died for sins once for all, the just for the unjust in order that He might bring us to God."[19]

Fourth, we must appropriate God's gift by personally accepting what Christ has done for us. One of the most familiar verses in the Bible says, "For God so loved the world, that he gave his only begotten Son, that whosoever believes in him should not perish, but have eternal life."[20]

Fifth, God wants each person to know His peace and be certain of his or her position before God, both now and for eternity. God's word says, "These things I have written to you who believe in the name of the Son of God, in order that *you may know* that you have eternal life."[21]

If you have not experienced the peace that comes through knowing God's forgiveness or have uncertainty regarding the future, consider Christ's provision as briefly described above. You can have his remedy by merely asking him. You can know that you are going to heaven.

About the Author

The author was raised in a Christian home but did not take his spiritual life seriously until he met some individuals involved in an organization called the Navigators in the eleventh grade. Upon graduation from high school, he moved to Oceanside, California, sharing the gospel and discipleship principles with marines heading for the battlefields of Korea. He later joined the Navy and became an electronics technician first class. Finally, ready to take studying seriously, he went to Los Angeles City College, was given a full academic scholarship to the University of Southern California, and graduated from George Washington Medical School. He had an internship and residencies and later a practice in both internal medicine and psychiatry. He was an assistant clinical professor at UCLA.

For decades he was active in leadership at Rolling Hills Covenant Church. He has had a keen interest in missions, has served on four mission boards, and has been involved and led a number of short-term mission trips. He has taught in the United States and overseas on a variety of subjects involving spiritual and psychological issues. He is the author of nine previous books.

He married Betty Harms in 1959, and they had two children, Susan and Greg, and have one granddaughter, Charissa. Betty and Dwight lived primarily in the greater Los Angeles area. Later, they moved to a retirement community which they both enjoyed until the sudden home going of Betty in 2013.

Endnotes

1   See 2 Corinthians 2:11

2   "US drone strikes kill 28 unknown people for every intended target, new Reprieve report reveals," *Reprieve.org*, accessed October 19, 2015, http://www.reprieve.org/us-drone-strikes-kill-28-unknown-people-for-every-intended-target-new-reprieve-report-reveals.html.

3   The scribe of these *missives* went on his computer browser and typed in "porn," and up popped the notation that there were 182 million sites available to click on. He did not want any of them to send future e-mails to him, so he closed it down. Several weeks later he was with a "dedicated Christian" who works in the computer/Internet field who volunteered he had a problem with porn, and he said there are many more sites available than that!

4   An advertisement in *Christianity Today*, May 2015, stating as its source "Pure Desire Ministries, 'PORN Usage in Evangelical Churches" (2009).

5   Quote attributed to Bill Perkins; original source unknown.

6   That elder is the scribe of these missives, and that statement was a major stimulus for writing this book.

7   Research performed by the Barna Group in 2014: http://www.covenanteyes.com/resources/download-your-copy-of-the-pornography-statistics-pack/, accessed 10/29/15. See also *The Porn Phenomenon, The Impact of Pornography in the Digital Age,* research commissioned by Josh McDowell Ministry, research conducted by Barna Group. Copyright 2016.

8   An advertisement in *Christianity Today*, May 2015 stating as its source "Pure Desire Ministries, 'PORN Usage in Evangelical Churches" (2009).

9   http://www.foxnews.com/us/2015/07/28/university-california-offers-six-choices-for-gender-identity.html; accessed 5/8/16.

10 http://www.usnews.com/news/articles/2015/09/03/obamacare-expands-rights-for-transgender-patients; accessed 5/9/16.

11 http://www.newsweek.com/what-ever-happened-sin-185180; accessed 2/13/16.

12 2 Chronicles 7:14 KJV

13 When I was nine years old I stuck my neck in a tent meeting and heard a traveling evangelist graphically describing hell, and I promptly left—how long he continued on this subject, I don't know. Since writing these missives, a friend of mine who was reading these missives loaned me a CD of a local pastor who did preach a sermon on heaven and another one on hell. I commend the pastor.

14 Adapted from "There's Something I've Wanted to Tell You" by Dwight L. Carlson, MD, copyright by Christian Medical & Dental Society, 1983.

15 Jeremiah 31:3

16 John 10:10

17 Isaiah 53:6

18 Romans 3:10–12

19 1 Peter 3:18

20 John 3:16

21 1 John 5:13, italics added

Printed in the United States
By Bookmasters